3

To my

MW01629017

from Ranulph Dyg, N.A.

Nov. 15, 2000

Ranulph Bye N.A.

RANULPH BYE'S

Collection of Old Firehouses

text by

RANULPH BYE

published by

The author and Mr. Charles E. Sigety

To the wonderful firemen
I met while doing this book,
as well as all firemen everywhere.

Library of Congress Catalogue Card Number 00-191528
ISBN # 0-9704040-0-X
Published by Ranulph Bye & Charles E. Sigety
Designed by Charles Grasse
Ploughman Publishing
Printed in the U.S.A.

Contents

7
Preface

8
Acknowledgements

9
Introduction

10
Fighting Fire

77
List of Works

Preface

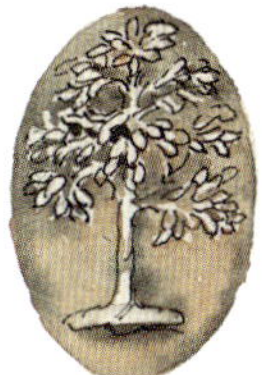

One might call this a sequel to my books VICTORIAN SKETCHBOOK and THE VANISHING DEPOT, published in 1980 and 1983. Although I had painted a few firehouses back in the eighties as a matter of pictorial interest, I had no idea that I would develop this subject seriously until a year and a half ago. As mentioned in VICTORIAN SKETCHBOOK, a firehouse or station (as it is sometimes called) was a structure of unique architectural style — different from a R.R. station, an office building, a private home or a post office.

This project was an adventure for me and an enjoyable one at that, like going on a treasure hunt. Although every town in America has a fire station, most are very plain buildings with three, four or five garage doors covered with a flat roof. This is not what I was looking for ... I discovered some firehouses have functional design, architectural embellishments, creative brickwork and towers for drying hoses that are built into the structure. In many cases, such as in towns and cities, a firehouse looks very much like a house, but with a large garage on the street side.

This writing can be described as an architectural study of firehouses found at random in eight eastern states plus a few more elsewhere. I will give a brief history of firefighting over the past 200 years. Otherwise, this a plain and simple picture book done in watercolor.

Ranulph Bye
February 2000

Acknowledgements

There are a number of people I want to thank who showed an interest in my project by providing me with locations and material of certain firehouses. They are: Mr. Ed McCarron, Roy Breg, my daughter Barbara Bye, my son Steve Bye and Shirley Cowper. And to my sister, Margaret Richie, who offered her expertise and knowledge on architecture. To my wife Glenna who gave me support from the beginning and accompanied me on a number of research trips.

I appreciate receiving permission from the MBI Publishing Co. to use excerpts from their book THE AMERICAN FIRE HOUSE by Gerry and Janet Souter. I also want to mention the Kerper Studio of photography for producing the transparencies used for color separation.

Also to the Spruance Library of the Mercer Museum which supplied me with information on American Fire Marks.

Also thanks to Charles Grasse who designed the book and supervised the production.

Lastly, I am deeply grateful to my friend Charles Sigety that, without his support, this book could not have been published.

INTRODUCTION

This endeavor has enabled me to take special trips to remote areas to seek out these buildings or follow-up on suggestions given to me by friends. This practice was not always satisfactory; one person's idea of a good subject was not always my choice. I alone would have to make the final judgement. In my experience I found the best firehouses would be found in the central sections of large towns or cities, not in the suburbs. This is where the older ones exist. I was told that in the five boroughs of New York City there exist around 125 firehouses, both old and new. Some are hard to find and may be sitting within a block of townhouses, concealed from view. I have illustrated three in Manhattan, each one very different from the other.

As a matter of principle, I have tried to find as many different styles of firehouses as possible in the limited space required. One thing they all have in common is the American flag displayed either on a pole nearby or from the building itself. And, of course, the large doors or bays which house the equipment usually face the street.

Some of the most picturesque firehouses I have found are now museums; they are no longer in service but they exhibit a lot of the paraphernalia once used by firemen. The steam pumper is an amazing piece of machinery. The steam fire engines, weighing as much as four tons, were pulled to fires by horses, which were well trained and loved by the firemen. Then came chemical engines and eventually motorized apparatus after 1920.

A few words about the interiors of firehouses. In the old days and up to the present time, accommodations for firemen to rest or sleep were available in the upstairs rooms. In large urban centers such as Philadelphia and New York, paid fire departments are the norm. That is not the case in smaller towns around the country where fire departments remain entirely volunteer. Most large companies employ a dispatcher who would receive fire calls. If calls came in, the men upstairs would quickly dress and slide down a pole to the ground floor to avoid delay.

*Time hung heavy around a firehouse. In the earliest professional days only one 24 hour day a month was off duty. The men lived, ate and passed their time waiting for a call. Banjos and guitars would be plucked and songs of great fires would be sung.

One of the areas of creative expression in the living quarters was cooking. Although neighbors and friends supplied hot meals, the firefighters also cooked from a common larder prepared for by the men. Meals would be wrought from the simplest ingredients. Any man who showed unusual skill with a pot was immediately protected by his companions.*

*Adapted from plaques at the firemens Hall Museum, 2nd and Quarry Sts., Philadelphia.

Engine house was a club room and had to be kept in order. Firemen would be expected to keep their engine in tip-top condition, well polished and wheels oiled. Being a member of a fire company was a steppingstone to political success.

I grew up as a boy in Holicong, Pa. Operating a volunteer fire company was an expensive business. In order to raise funds, The Midway Volunteer Fire Co. organized Carnivals usually held every summer for two weeks. Over the years, money earned would be used to build a new firehouse, purchase ground for carnivals and buy new pumper equipment. At the time of this writing, the purchase of a new pumper is estimated at a cost of $150,000. To run a fully paid fire company taking into account equipment replacement and repairs, it costs upwards of $1.5 million a year.

*For years, Americans have been entranced by the romance, the lore and the legend of fire-fighting, from tales of early bucket brigades to eyewitness accounts of city-wide conflagrations. Since the organization of the country's first volunteer fire company, the Union in Philadelphia in 1736, the saga of fire fighters has grown epic. The city's earliest fire companies included the Fellowship (1756), the Hibernia (1752), the Northern Liberties (1756), The King George the Third (1761), The Harmony (1784), the Good Will (1802), and the Neptune Hose Company (1805). It was not long until artists began depicting the work of fire fighters racing to a fire, battling the blaze, saving a child, and returning home. By the third-quarter of the nineteenth century, such scenes were being mass-produced by lithographers, the most familiar of which, Currier and Ives, issued an entire series entitled THE LIFE OF A FIREMAN.

**With minor variations, the houses were two or three-story brick or frame structures with one bay. The second floor was a dormitory for men and the rear of the first floor served as a stable area for the horses.

Some of the houses built after the Chicago Fire have architectural merit including layered brickwork, cornices, bay windows, and cut stone decoration but inside they remained virtually unchanged. While many firehouses were built on corner lots, the era of the "storefront" house shoehorned into a business block had come to stay in cities across the country. These houses usually tried to blend in with the architecture of the flanking structures, often matching the older marble and stone carvings of their neighbors with less expensive cast-iron facades bolted to the bricks.

The competition between volunteer companies had also extended to firehouse design. This "our house is grander than yours" attitude continued in smaller cities and towns through the turn of the century while large cities chose uniformity in design when possible, small towns turned to their business communities for funds, or the volunteers themselves passed the hat. Communities competing to build the most elegant firehouses and the communities themselves choosing to focus their civic pride on the sumptuousness of their public buildings — notably the firehouse — was an escalation of self consciousness that rode the architectural high road.

*From THE AMERICAN FIRE STATION by Gerry and Janet Souter
**From Pennsylvania HERITAGE, SUMMER

FIGHTING FIRE

Benjamin Franklin, who originally came from Boston, noted that the residents of Philadelphia, which he adopted, were less prepared to fight fires, so he consulted the Junto, a benevolent group dedicated to civic and self-improvement, and asked for suggestions on better ways to fight fires.

Franklin also sought ways to improve fire-fighting techniques. In an article of the PENNSYLVANIA GAZETTE of 1773 it was noted how fires were being fought in Philadelphia. There was little organization and men of all ages and professions volunteered to fight fires.

Goodwill and amateur firefighters were not enough. So Franklin suggested to create clubs of active men to attend all fires whenever they happen. Franklin, who owned the GAZETTE, wrote anonymous letters admonishing citizens to be more careful around the house where coal stoves were the norm in heating.

He urged that chimney sweeps should be licensed by the city and be held responsible for their work. In Boston, a society of active men belonged to each fire engine, whose business is to attend all fires whenever they happen. Under Franklin, a group of thirty men came together to form the Union Fire Company on December 7, 1736. In those days leather buckets were used to fight fires and blaze battlers met monthly to talk about fire prevention. It was mandatory that home owners have fire buckets in their houses.

In Philadelphia other men were desirous of joining the Union, but were urged to form their own fire companies. Within a short time several other fire companies organized separate fire clubs including the Heart-In Hand, the Britannia, the Fellowship, as well as several other fire companies.

Under the leadership of Benjamin Franklin, Philadelphia became one of the safest cities in terms of fire damage.

Benjamin Franklin, in Philadelphia, founded the first volunteer fire company in 1736 and established the first fire insurance company called "Hand-In-hand". Legend has it that George Washington was an active volunteer fire fighter and a member of the Friendship Fire Company of Alexandria, Virginia, although there is no written record to prove it.

When fire broke out in Philadelphia, in the nineteenth century, it was the volunteers, not professional firefighters, who quelled the blaze. From 1800 until 1871, the year when a paid, professional department replaced volunteers. Philadelphia's fire companies learned to express widely held ideals of civic responsibility and masculine virtue through the fighting of fires.

*Philadelphia's Volunteer Fire Companies were replaced by a paid department in 1871. In 1875, the survivors formed the Volunteer Firemens Association to commemmorate their service and pay benefits to relatives when members died.

Between 1875 and 1919 the V.F.A. marched in parades, traveled to visit brother firemen in other cities and collected mementoes of the old Volunteer department. Its members re-fought the fires of their youth, talked politics, smoked cigars, toasted each other at balls and dinners, and grew nostalgic. They lovingly restored their parade engine and hose carriage, and debated the proper treatment of relics in their possession. Their motto "MANY HAPPY DAYS" seemed to ignore the conflict and controversies that had once marked the volunteer service.

*Printed at Fireman's exhibit at Mercer Museum 1999.

MDCCCXV
Ranulph Bye, NA.

Left ENGINE HOUSE, 1600 Block of Belmont Ave., Philadelphia, PA. I came upon this firehouse quite by accident, no one had told me about it. I found it to be an extraordinary building but it had gone into disrepair. The bay on the left had been boarded up, so I restored it to match the one still visible. A distinctive feature of this firehouse is a plaque or bas-relief seal of the city of Philadelphia. Date in Roman numerals reads 1895. Romanesque windows and corner quoins identify this structure as more than ordinary. A separate study is shown on the following page.

Center Detail of Philadelphia Coat of Arms.

Above REED STREET ENGINE HOUSE, 1894, Between Delaware Avenue and Front Street, Philadelphia. Ironically, the Reed Street Engine House, which like most Victorian structures, was built to last, now struggles to survive in a wasteland near dock-lined Delaware River front. To come upon it brings culture shock. There are Jacobean details in the curvilinear and stepped gables and in the tall, corbelled chimney. When you add the polygonal, crenelated tower to the total image, it reads as from the distant past. This aristocratic engine house is an expression in the Queen Anne Mode.

Rows of precision-cut sawtooth bricks create horizontal bands or belt courses; this and other refinements such as the design-conscious window arrangement, should help stimulate a re-use of this structure.

Despite its atmosphere of romance, the architectural components fitted the nineteenth century firehouse function with economy. Even the tower was essential, serving to dry the long wet hoses hauled up by block and tackle.

The small houses are gone now, the trees leveled, the elevated expressway I-95 carries heavy traffic through south Philadelphia. Reed Street Engine House stands isolated and mute.*

*From VICTORIAN SKETCHBOOK by Bye and Richie 1980.

Ranulph Bye

Top Left LADDER 16 ENGINE NO. 6, Belgrade and Huntington Sts., Philadelphia, PA 1875. This building is one of the most visually gratifying firehouses in the city. The architects have made an effort to build a dignified structure. The elegeant cornice work and Balustrade above it creates this effect. As can be observed in the illustration the firehouse is located in a section of row houses in North Philadelphia, and it stands out as something important.

Bottom ENGINE HOUSE No. 8, FIREMENS MUSEUM, 147 No. 2nd Street, Philadelphia, PA. In this view we are looking east at the front of the firehouse. The Benj. Franklin Memorial bridge can be seen in the background on the right. In actuality, the bridge should appear on the left but for compositional reasons, I switched it with the Victorian house on the left which seemed to fit nicely in the design.

Above WASHINGTON HOSE COMPANY NO. 1, Conshohocken, PA. Built in 1874 on Fayette Street, this firehouse is no longer in service but is listed on The National Register of Historic Places. Recognized for its important architectural statement, it was spared when the surrounding neighborhood was demolished in the 1950s.

Above BRISTOL FIRE COMPANY NO. 1, Market and Woods Streets, Bristol, PA. Bristol is Bucks County's largest town and one of the oldest boroughs in the state. The town was laid out in 1697. Fire stations were first suggested (or recommended) by Benjamin Franklin, but not until the 1740s or 1750s, hence any early stations would have been dated after the mid-18th century, wherever they may be.

Bristol is located on the Delaware River about twenty miles above Philadelphia. A Friends Meeting stands across the street.

Right DOYLESTOWN FIRE COMPANY NO. 1, Doylestown, PA, with 1923 Ahrens-Fox Fire Pumper. The Doylestown Fire Engine Co. was organized Jan. 24, 1825, at the house of Jacob Kohl. It was later renamed the Friendship Fire Co. in 1834.

In 1893 a new fire department, called The Doylestown Fire Co., was organized. The Shewell Ave. lot was purchased in 1902.

There were a number of serious fires in Doylestown to houses, mills, barns and small factories but, for the most part, Doylestown has escaped very destructive fires up until 1900.

FIRE CO No 1
Ranulph Bye N.A.

Above ALARM RING, Point Pleasant Fire Co., Point Pleasant, PA. Once used to alert firemen in case of fire, they are now no longer used but have become a momento and lawn ornament of a bygone era.

Right FIREHOUSE ROADSIDE MARKER, Carversville, PA. These markers can be seen anywhere in Pennsylvania to warn motorists that a firehouse is in the immediate area.

Ranulph Bye

EAGLE . FIRE CO.
Ranulph Bye, MA

Left EAGLE FIRE COMPANY, New Hope, PA. Dedicated October 17, 1908; organized 1812. The residents of Lambertville and New Hope recognized the threat that fire posed to their homes and so from the inception of organized firefighting in both towns, the fire companies have always been staffed by willing and loyal volunteers. It was in everyone's interest to take the risk of fire very seriously.

The Eagle Fire Company of New Hope was for many years the only fire company for both villages. It is the oldest fire company in Bucks County and among the first fire companies in the nation. In this view we see the original firehouse located in the center of town. A new larger facility has been built on Route 202 just on the outskirts of town.

Above MIDWAY FIRE COMPANY, Lahaska, PA. The large stone building on the left was once a meeting house belonging to Buckingham Friends Meeting. The Quakers were divided in 1828 into two factions, The Hicksite and the Orthodox. Each faction had its own place of worship. When Friends decided to unify, the two groups left one building vacant. Henceforth the Midway Fire Company offered to purchase it. It is a beautiful example of early American Colonial architecture with shuttered windows and hoods over entrance doors. The new bays for equipment were later added next door.

Because of its central location between the fire companies in Doylestown and New Hope, it was decided to call the new company the Midway Volunteer Fire Company. The date was 1931.

This painting is selected as a memorial to FRANK BIANCO who was a long time volunteer of the fire company.

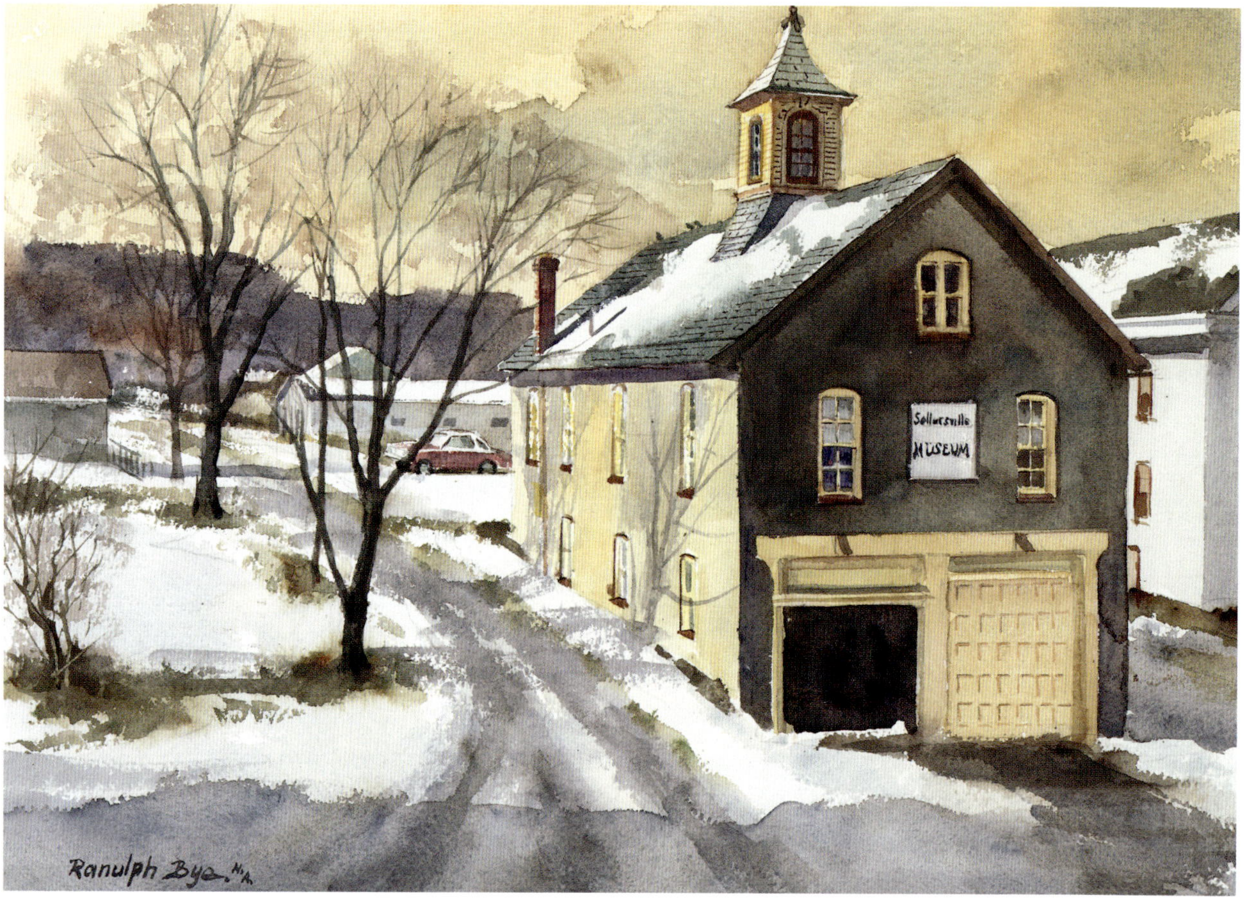

STOP
PERKASIE
Ranulph Bye, NA.

Top Left SELLERSVILLE VOLUNTEER FIRE CO., Sellersville, PA, instituted 1888. Once a barn and remodeled into a firehouse, this building is now a museum having outgrown this facility. It is simply a utilitarian building with no need to be pretentious.
Bottom PERKASIE FIREHOUSE, Perkasie, Bucks County, PA. Brick structure with two bays. The four rounded windows and round gable helps to create some design in an otherwise mundane firehouse.
Above PHILA. STEAM FIRE COMPANY NO. 1, Pottstown, PA. Erected in 1871, this firehouse is similar to the one in Norristown. Upstairs is a large area for sleeping accommodation and recreation.

NO TURN ON RED
LAUREL
Ranulph Bye

Left LAUREL FIRE COMPANY NO. 1, York, PA. The Laurel Fire Company was organized February 13, 1790, at a meeting held at the home of Abraham Miller. It was agreed that the company "shall be stiled the Laurel Fire Company." A device for making fire buckets was approved and a committee named to make fire hooks and ladders.

The story of the Laurel is the story of York. Down through the years, the history of the company is intertwined and inter-mingled with the civic and religious life of the community. While the company, under its present corporate title, dates its existence from the year 1790, there is ample evidence in the written history of the city and the records of the company to link the Laurel directly with the earlier Sun Fire Company of Yorktown.

Besides safeguarding the community the company has always taken an active part in the promotion of social and civic celebrations of varied types. Balls, picnics, festivals, entertainments and benefit performances are included in a long list of activities.

About the building, it is a beauty to behold and shows many fine features of Victorian style.

Top Right FIRE BELL, York County Fire Museum. A detail study of the fire bell on the lawn of the York County Fire Museum. It is a memorial to a fire horse. In the background is a memorial to the firemen of the former Royal Fire Station No. 6.

Ranulph Bye

Left ROYAL FIRE STATION NO. 6, York, PA. *Funded by private businessmen, Royal Fire Station No. 6 was a state-of-the-art red brick fire barn when it opened for business in 1903 at York, Pennsylvania. Its beautifully maintained interior is now the York County Fire Museum and displays a complete collection of firefighting apparatus and artifacts. This was probably the last of the opulent volunteer houses built with private money.

On the front lawn you will see a painted statue of a fireman standing high on a pedestal amidst a thicket of trees. The fireman carries a child in one arm and a lantern in the other. (See detailed illustration.)

The museum is located at the edge of a neighborhood of light industry and low-income housing. You don't see any graffiti or defacement in any way. This building and the grounds around it is a tribute to York's volunteer firemen, alive and dead, who gave their best to the city. In front of the museum is a large fire bell with an inscription stating "Old Joe/Union Steam Fire Engine Number 3/AD 1884. (See detailed painting.)

Royal Engine No. 6 is a men's club that also happens to be a firehouse. It was probably the last of its kind as volunteer stations became more rare in the cities when operating budgets slimmed down.*

*From THE AMERICAN FIRE STATION by Gerry and Janet Souter.

Above UNION FIRE COMPANY NO. 1, Carlisle, Pennsylvania 1869. *The house uses cut stone, terra cotta, and prestamped brick as decoration across its facade and tower for a three-dimension effect topped by a wood cupola and bell. These design touches announced the coming trend of Victorian mixing of textures and materials that would achieve full flower in the 1880s thru the turn of the century.

*From THE AMERICAN FIRE STATION by Gerry and Janet Souter.

Above HOOK AND LADDER NO. 1, Reading, PA, Second and Penn Street. The Queen Anne style building is now a restaurant but still called "THE FIREHOUSE". Built around 1890's, it is one of several firehouses in this large industrial city; most of more recent vintage. Note the handsome cupola and the elegant lamppost.

Top Right ENGINE 803, TREMONT FIRE COMPANY, Tremont, PA. Tremont is a small town located in the heart of the Appalachian Mountains on Route 209 between Pottsville and Millersburg. As you can see the firehouse is "shoehorned" between two houses on Main Street. I liked the scallopped frieze above the second floor windows; unusual for a country station. Date is about 1897.

Bottom DAUNTLESS HOOK AND LADDER COMPANY, Selinsgrove, PA. Organized 1874. Selinsgrove is located on the west bank of the Susquehanna River about 37 miles above Harrisburg. It has more character than most firehouses in the region, although it looks more like an industrial shop than a firehouse. The structure on top of the gable is a siren.

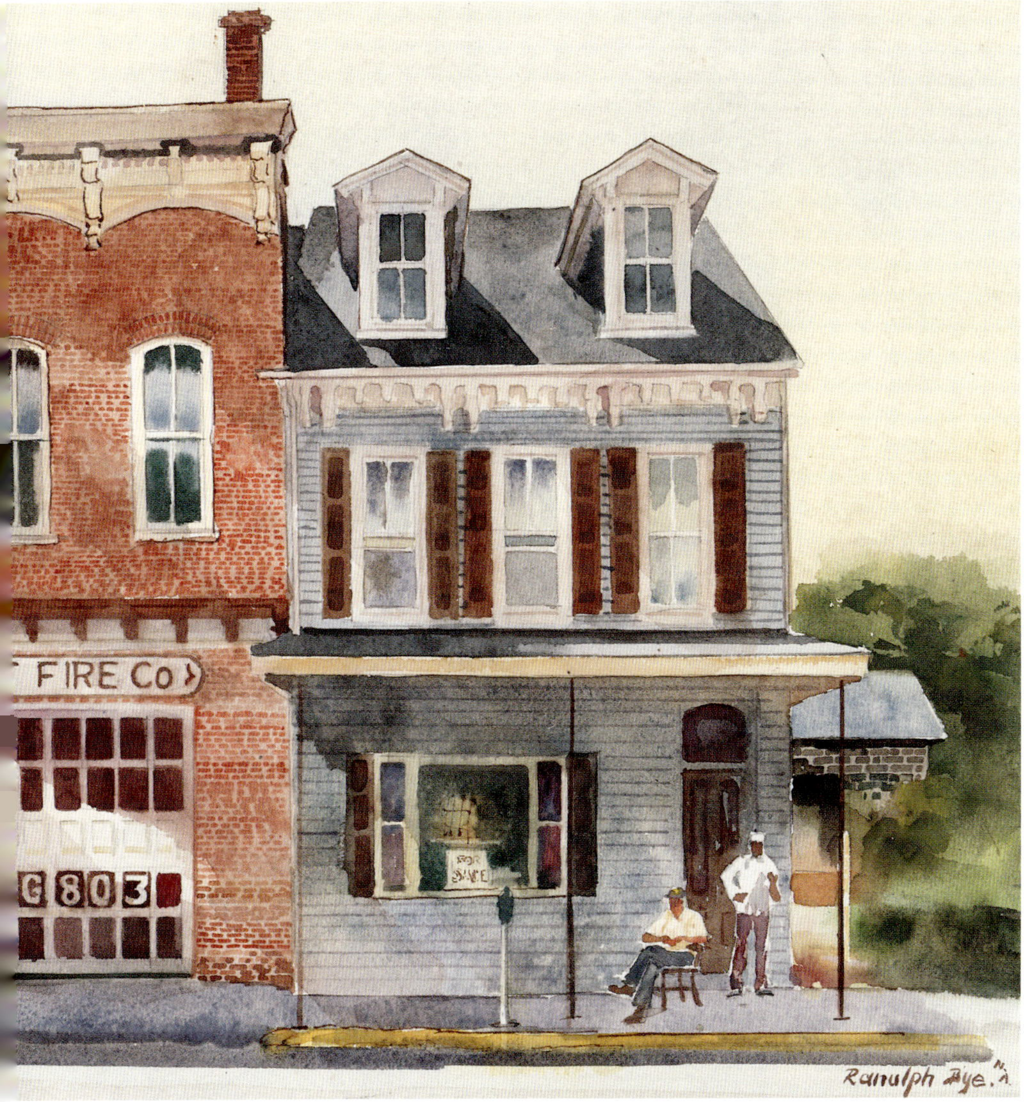

DAUNTLESS HOOK & LADDER FIRE COMPANY
COMPANY 80
Ranulph Bye

WASHINGTON FIRE CO.
Ranulph Bye, N.A.

Left WASHINGTON FIRE COMPANY NO. 1, Centre Street, Ashland, PA. This firehouse seems to have a lot of charm with its colorful bell tower and twin gabled house next door. The company was organized in 1870.

Above CITIZENS ENGINE HOUSE NO. 2, South Williamsport, PA. American firehouse builders show independence of taste and design as evidenced in this industrial neighborhood. Date is around 1880-1890.

Above SHARTLESVILLE FIREHOUSE, PA. Date unknown but it's evident that this firehouse is a conversion from a back yard outbuilding.

Right MARION HOSE COMPANY, NO. 1, on Upper Broadway, Jim Thorpe, PA. Formerly named Mauch Chunk, the town was renamed Jim Thorpe to honor a famous athlete of American Indian stock. Because of the rugged topography, the town is divided into three sections each with its own firehouse. Jim Thorpe is noted for its fine Victorian homes, among them the residence of Asa Packer who founded the Lehigh Valley railroad. He built a large Italianate style mansion overlooking the Lehigh River which is now a museum. He also built another mansion in second empire style for his son, Harry. The Lehigh Coal and Navigation Co. had its main office in Jim Thorpe. It shipped coal coming down from the mines above it, then transported it via canal barges down to the large industrial cities of Allentown and Bethlehem.

In this painting, the firehouse butts up against a wooded cliff behind it and a movie theatre on the right.

MARION·HOSE·CO·No1
Ranulph Bye, N.A.

MARION FIRE Co
STOUCHSBURG
Ranulph Bye

Left MARION FIRE COMPANY, Stouchsburg, PA. A quiet town in Marion Township, Lancaster County, of about 200 homes and businesses west of Womelsdorf, Rt. 422. Farms and cornfields butt up against main street houses. An attempt is made to create dignity by adding a cupola to an otherwise simply designed brick firehouse.

Above ANTHRACITE FIRE COMPANY, Mt. Carmel, PA, 1882. Located in the coal region of eastern Pennsylvania, this firehouse and the one in Ashland are particularly significant where one does not find architecture in the grand style. This firehouse is an exceptionally fine building. The tiled roof is Hispanic and the rounded windows above the bays are well proportioned. The skirted wings with columned lanterns give an elegant touch.

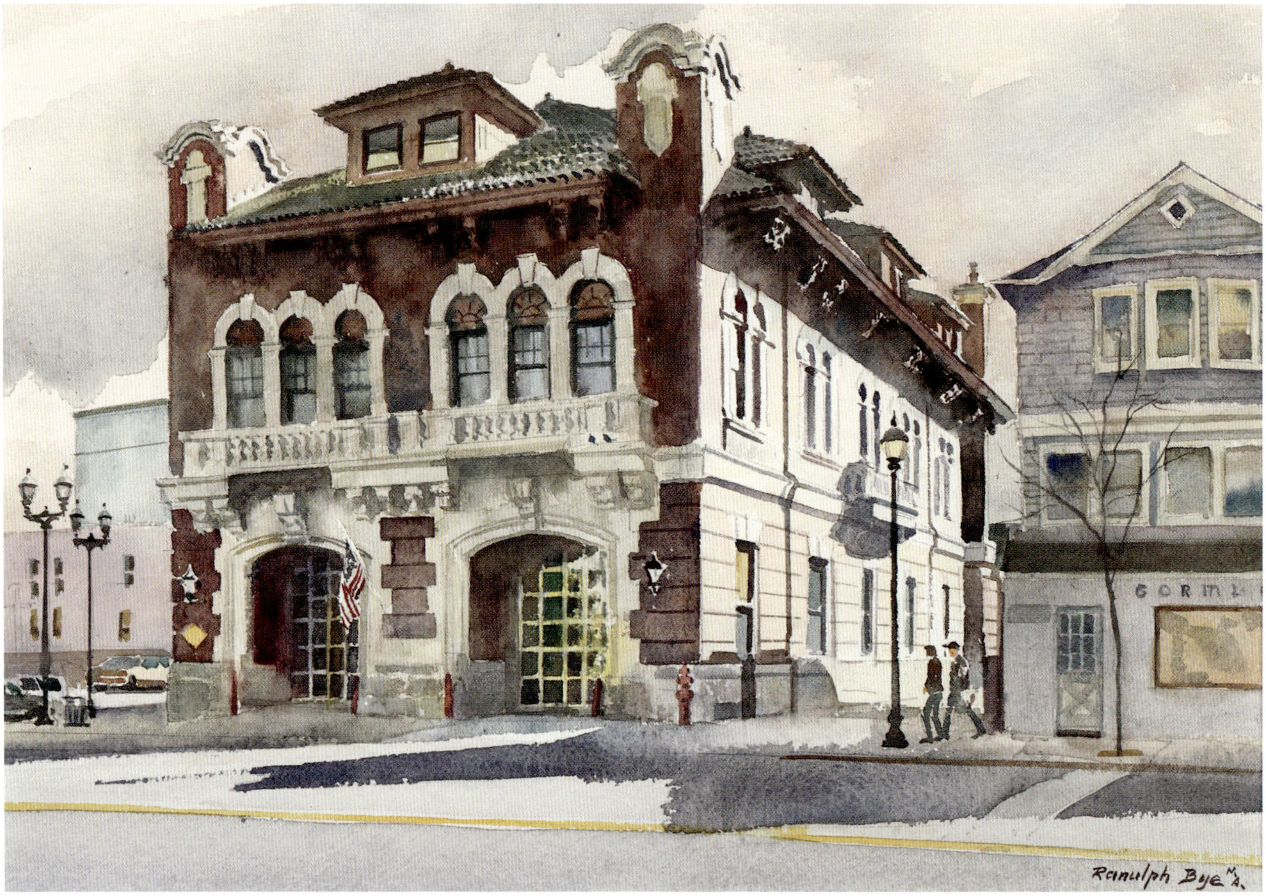

Ranulph Bye N.A.

RELIEF 2 HOSE
Ranulph Bye N.A.

Top Left ENGINE NO. 4; TRUCK NO. 4, ATLANTIC CITY FIRE DEPT., Atlantic City, NJ. Pretentious is the key word here. It seems that the fire company is displaying the towns' importance as a famous resort and playground center. This firehouse is in the grand style.

Bottom Left RELIEF HOSE COMPANY NO. 2, Raritan, NJ. A nice example of a single bay engine house with hose drying tower attached.

Above CAPE MAY FIRE MUSEUM, Cape May, NJ. Reconstructed in 1984. It's a delight to come upon this charming firehouse in a town noted for its fine collection of Victorian homes. A new modern facility has been erected nearby.

FIREMAN'S MUSEUM

Somerville relies upon volunteers to staff its Fire Department. The first volunteer fire company organized in 1835. Since then, three more companies have formed, all manned by volunteers.

This building was constructed in 1888 for the West End Hose Company to meet the needs of residents on the west side of town. The new brick building replaced a wooden shed which had housed the hand-drawn fire fighting apparatus of Union Fire Co. No. 1 (1852-1878). Some of the bricks used in the construction were acquired when Daniel Robert demolished the "castle" on the site now occupied by Borough Hall. In addition to Hand drawn fire apparatus, the building was home to the Borough's first horse drawn truck (1888) and Macky, the horse purchased to pull the single harness rig. Later, in 1916, the first motorized apparatus was purchased for West End Hose Company.

In 1970, West End Hose relocated to High Street. The original firehouse was dedicated as a museum to all of the men who have served in the Somerville Fire Department.

Top Left WEST END HOSE COMPANY, 1888, NOW FIREMENS MUSEUM, Somerville, NJ. Plaque on building reads as follows: *Center* Somerville relies on volunteers to staff its fire dept. First volunteer fire company organized in 1835. Since then, three more companies have formed, all maned by volunteers. This building was constructed in 1888 for the West End Hose Company to meet the needs of residents on the west side of town. The new building replaced a wooden shed which had housed the hand-drawn fire fighting apparatus of Union Fire Co. No. 1 (1852-1878). In 1916 the first motorized apparatus was purchased for the West End Hose Co.

Bottom FREEHOLD FIRE DEPARTMENT, Freehold, NJ. Organized April 20, 1872. Greek Revival is the key word here, and a fine example as well. The semi-lunar Oculus in the gable and cupola above enhance the composition. I enjoyed including the old R.R. Station in the background.

Above *FIRE HEADQUARTERS at South Orange, NJ. Despite the leaps and bounds that technology was making in the private and business sector of America, fire departments were rooted in tradition. Fathers passed along the torch to sons, and fire chiefs stayed on with their ideas about how a fire should be fought for decades after improved methods were available. Horses were still on fire department rosters years and years after gasoline-powered fire engines were hard at work. Steam-powered pumpers still hunkered at the back of the engine floor in reserve as late as the 1940's.

A notable example of this far-down-the-road transition is the Fire Headquarters in South Orange, NJ. On Feb. 25, 1925, the sum of $70,000 was appropriated for the construction of a firehouse. Architects, Dillon and Beadel, came up with a design that stands today as a beautiful interpretation of the Norman style.

Offices are housed in the turret to the left of the three main bays. That feature balanced the 90-foot hose-drying tower to the right of the bays. The building was designed without a kitchen. This was because the paid men were given three one-hour dinner times on a rotating basis to leave the firehouse and return. After a disastrous fire, a whole new shift was added and the kitchen was built where the horse stalls were originally designed to be built.

*After THE AMERICAN FIRE STATION by Gerry and Janet Souter.

J.C.F.D.
TRUCK No 4
1894
FORT
APACHE
F.D.J.C.
FIRST
AID
AME
FRUITS VEGETABL
Free Do
Ranulph Bye, N.A.

Left JERSEY CITY FIRE DEPARTMENT, TRUCK NO. 4, Jersey City, NJ. Built in 1894, this engine house is one of the most richly embellished buildings in this collection. The facade contains many of the elements in this Queen Anne revival interpretation. The result is quite eclectic. When I came upon this firehouse in the winter of '98. I was dumbfounded by what I saw.

Above HOOK AND LADDER NO. 3, Central Ave., Jersey City, NJ. Jersey City is fortunate in having some distinctive firehouse designs located throughout the city. The title seems too bold a statement; however, the rounded windows, columns and heavy cornice display dignity to the facade.

Bottom ENGINE COMPANY NO. 5, 278 Sixth Street, Jersey City, NJ. I came upon this firehouse quite by accident while driving around Jersey City. I was struck by its brilliant red door which I found difficult to reproduce in water color. The distinguishing architectural feature is the pediment gable over the second floor and repeated over the windows beneath it. As is so often the case, there was no one around to inquire about its date and history. This building is now a studio residence.

Above HOBOKEN LADDER COMPANY, The Island, Observer Highway, Hoboken, NJ. An unusual feature of this firehouse is that equipment can drive right through from the rear. It was built in 1892.

Right FIRE STATION AND TOWN HALL, Bordentown, NJ. Bordentown: This extraordinary architectural gem is basically Greek Revival (1830-1860). The hose tower, belfry, clock and balcony, integrated with the rest of the building, come across as a tour de force of the architect, offering a pleasing addition to the built environment of the town.

1752
RELIEF
1892
1
1892
Ranulph Bye

Left RELIEF FIRE ENGINE COMPANY NO. 1, 1892, Mount Holly, NJ. The lower bulk of this 1892 Relief Engine House comes at you with the monumentality of H.H. Richardson of Trinity Church, Boston. The sum of this building with its merry-go-round belfry, its lattice work and knobbed finials brings pleasure to the eye. This engine house is the oldest volunteer fire company in continued service in the United States. In order to preserve its identity, the company changed its name twice; first, after the Revolution from Brittania Fire Company (no longer appropriate) to Mt. Holly Fire Company, and second, in order to avoid confusion with another company of the name, to Relief Fire Engine Company Number One.

Mt. Holly, county seat of Burlington, South Jersey, a rural town first settled in 1677, was home of John Woolman, an early Quaker abolitionist who attempted to win his point by sitting quietly, but indefinitely by a slave-holder's fireside.**

**From VICTORIAN SKETCHBOOK by Bye and Richie 1980.

Above ENGINE COMPANY NO. 5, Trenton, NJ, Willow Street. A simply constructed firehouse which could be found in any city.

Above FLEETWING FIRE COMPANY, Lambertville, NJ. Originally built in 1867, with later alterations. This is one of my favorite studies in the whole collection. I like the way the engine snuggles into the bay, so cozy. For a small city, Lambertville contains four separate fire companies, all volunteer. They are: the Hibernia, Columbia, the Union and Fleetwing, all one bay facilities and much the same in design with a large bay window on second floor topped by a heavy bracketed cornice. As of 1996, all four firehouses were still in operation.

Right HIBERNIA FIRE HOUSE, Lambertville, NJ. See caption on Fleetwing Firehouse, Lambertville. Four fire stations are similar. This one is built along Swan Creek on the south side of town.

EDGEWATER VOLUNTEER
FIRE DEPT. CO. No 1
Ranulph Bye NA.

Left EDGEWATER VOLUNTEER FIRE DEPT. NO. 1, Edgewater, NJ. A charming one bay firehouse with a Dutch style stepped gable and finial on top.
Above FIREHOUSE, Phillipsburg, NJ. Less ornate than many, this is a simply designed firehouse of Romanesque influence and well suited for its environment.

PETERS SPRINGS
FIRE MUSEUM
BALTIMORE
6

Above BALTIMORE CITY FIRE MUSEUM: ENGINE NO. 6, Gay and Ensor Streets. Located in an old firehouse built in 1853 which includes an extended tower for a night watchman who scanned the skyline for signs of fire. The tower is 117 feet tall and includes Gothic style windows super-imposed on the Italianate style tower modeled after Giotto's Campanile in Florence, Italy.

Left JUNIOR FIRE CO. NO. 2, Frederick, MD. This firehouse is located a few blocks north of the United Firehouse. The crenelated battlements on the tower is the distinctive feature of the firehouse. The street on which it stands shows typical homes of the mid-19th century. Additions and renovations were done in 1980-81.

Above UNITED FIRE COMPANY NO. 3, Market St. and All Saints St., Frederick, MD. This firehouse has an unusually attractive belfry and it's one of reasons I selected it for this collection. Organized 1848; rebuilt 1905.

Right ENGINE 55, 363 Broome Street, New York, NY. This is a particularly fine engine house in lower Manhattan with an assortment of architectural embellishments. Firemen that I have talked to are very proud of it.

55 ENGINE 55
365
Ranulph Bye

Above HOOK & LADDER NO. 8, Corner of Varick and Broome St., New York, NY. This engine house gives great charm, particularly because it is surrounded by a number of non-descript commercial buildings. The red door provides a delight to an otherwise somber scene. Hook and Ladder defines the apparatus which is equipped to reach high elevations in fighting a fire. The location is downtown Manhattan.

Right NEW YORK CITY FIRE DEPARTMENT, 163 East 67th Street, New York, NY, Engine Company 33; Ladder Company 16. As you can see in this painting, this firehouse is richly endowed with architectural embellishments which befits its location in an upscale neighborhood. In this painting, I could only render the first four floors; the building rises another two floors, topped by a three story ornate tower.

In the mid-19th century most of this block was owned by the city, and from 1886 to 1890 four buildings went up on the north side of the street. The first and biggest was the Fire Department headquarters at 157 East 67th St. Built in 1886 to take advantage of the strategic site on the brow of Lenox Hill – from the walkway at the top of the 150-foot-high tower, a lookout could see all the way down to the battery. According to a fire historian, other fire towers in the city were no longer used. Designed by Napoleon LeBrun, the Romantic-style building also housed the department's intricate telegraph system.

39 ENGINE COMPANY 39
16 LADDER COMPANY 16
FDNY
39
Ranulph Bye

Above ENGINE 4 FIREHOUSE, Elmira, NY. When I found this firehouse in the winter of February, 2000, it was in forlorn condition and badly in need of restoration which the city is planning to do. Never-the-less, it is a gem of a building and richly endowed with ornamentation — the use of stepped gables, quoins, finials, balustrades and decorative brickwork. The date stone on upper gable reads 1897.

Right KINGSTON, NEW YORK, Volunteer Firemen's Hall and Museum of Kingston, 365 Fair Street; Built 1857, Eagle Hose & Ladder No. 1; Washington No. 3. A well proportioned building with a bell tower breaking through the pediment. A pair of shuttered windows on second floor blends well with the total effect. An open belfry is clearly featured. The interior exhibits handdrawn parade carriage, motorized apparatus, a working Gamewell fire alarm system, uniforms, badges, old prints, books, documents and mugs.

Ranulph Bye

Above A.M. OSBORNE HOSE CO. NO. 2, Catskill, NY. A pair of bay windows on second floor is an unusual feature in this example.

Right BRICK FIREHOUSE, Catskill, NY. 1900 Now out of service, the interior contains a garment making shop.

1900
WINGS
Ranulph Bye

8
H.F.D.
8
8
J.W. HOYSRADT HOSE & CHEMICAL CO.
8
Ranulph Dye

Left J. W. HOYSRADT HOSE AND CHEMICAL CO. NO. 8, Hudson, NY 1925. For a small city there are a number of attractive firehouses placed around the town, like this one. Some are named after important officials from an earlier time.

Above C. H. EVANS FIRE COMPANY NO. 3, Hudson, NY 1888. As mentioned in the introduction, many firehouses in small towns tried to blend in with neighboring houses by using similar building materials and styles. Such is the case here.

2
2 H.W. ROGERS HOSE CO. 2
Ranulph Bye

Left H. W. ROGERS HOSE COMPANY NO. 2, Hudson, NY. This firehouse displays more elegance than some others in this village along the Hudson. Exquisitely molded window heads and frieze above are pure Victorian, and blends well with the houses next door. Here again, we have a good example of a firehouse wedged between two homes, a common practice in downtown areas.

Above CENTRAL FIRE STATION NO. 1, Cortland, NY. Originally built in 1914, this Cortland, New York, firehouse was revamped into its current appearance in 1927 by order of the town fathers. Listed on the National Register, its refurbished appearance in Dutch style houses Engine 1. The stepped gables are pure Dutch in origin and is exemplified in many public buildings throughout New York State.

Above ENGINE NO. 6, Waterbury, CT Established 1905 on Willow Street. This firehouse can be defined in possessing some important Greek features particularly in the entablature supported by two pairs of Ionic columns. The result is a formal dignified appearance. The single bay promotes a center of interest for the engine parked inside.

Right ENGINE COMPANY NO. 2, Seymour, Connecticut, Citizen Engine Co. No. 2 1882-1884. This is a striking building with a stepped gable over the engine bay and an imposing tower for drying hoses topped by an open belfry.

CITIZEN ENGINE CO.
NORWAY
MACK
Ranulph Bye N.A.

Ranulph Bye. MA.

Left WORCESTER FIRE DEPARTMENT, Worcester, MA. Although this station is still in service, a more modern facility has been built in another part of town. Built around 1895, this engine house befits a city of this size and importance. The facade is sumptuously designed with variegated glass windows, brackets set back of the central theme, arches, scrolls and balconies. The window areas are recessed from the front of the building which adds to the visual effect.

Above WORCESTER CENTRAL FIRE DIVISION, Worcester, Massachusetts, Commercial Street. This fire station was erected in 1974-75. It was selected not for any architectural virtue, but it is much better than most fire buildings built during this period. The use of quoins and a bullseye in the gable becomes window dressing. This facility can accommodate more equipment than the other fire stations included in this collection.

Above LOWELL FIRE DEPARTMENT, Lowell, MA, Built 1891 on Lawrence Street. Two bays to accommodate the apparatus and a pair of overhead bay windows turned a copper green. It seems this department has paid personnel who are on duty to receive calls.

Right TORRENT FIRE HOUSE, Lowell, MA (1877), Ladder No. 2, Branch St. Lowell, being a large town, has a number of substantial firehouses located in the metropolitan area. I selected two for this collection. All are quite different from each other. Torrent seems to have Colonial influence shown with a heavy bracketed gable.

TORRENT
Ranulph Bye N.A.

Above IPSWICH FIRE HOUSE, Ipswich, MA. A three bay engine house with rounded windows defines it as Romanesque. The building date would be in the 20's. Located on Route 133, about halfway between Newburyport and Gloucester.

Right MASSASOIT FIRE COMPANY, Damariscotta, ME, Circa 1870. This picturesque building is now an art gallery. The townspeople have taken pride in excellence and have harmonized this station with the building across the square.

THE FIREHOUSE

Above PARIS FIRE DEPARTMENT, Paris, ME. This firehouse is older than it appears, built 1900; located in southern Maine near the New Hampshire border… The four bays probably added on at a later date. Nicely placed in a grove of pines.

Right AUBURN ENGINE HOUSE, Spring and Court Sts., Auburn, ME. This engine house is placed on The National Register of Historic Places. This stolid building is in stern contrast, but still a foil, to the graceful church across the street.

ENGINE HOUSE
Ranulph Bye

Above THOMASTON FIRE COMPANY, Thomaston, ME. What are we seeing? A fire station in a colonial house. Probably, in the interest of economy the town's people acquired this house which offered the appropriate size and location to accommodate the equipment. The only exterior change required was to pierce the roof ridge for the hose-drying tower and the bellcote.

The entrance or vestibule is a modern addition needed for access to the present restaurant.

Right ENGINE HOUSE, Racine, WI. I came upon this firehouse on a trip to the middle west thirty-four years ago. I have no idea of its present use or condition, but by seeing its solid construction, it may last hundreds of years. It looks like a small castle with medieval battlements and a look-out tower; a most unique firehouse in this collection.

Ranulph Bye

Above ENGINE 24, Oakland, CA. This unusual creation was built in a residential neighborhood and neighbors labeled it "Mother Goose House". Opened in 1927, the landscaping has taken over what was once a simple ground cover.

This is an example of Home Firehouse Design so it would blend in with other homes down the street.

List of Works

PAGE #

2. Alarm Ring, Pt. Pleasant Fire Co., Point Pleasant, PA

3. *American Fire Mark, Pumper Firemens Insurance Co. of Baltimore (1825)

4. American Fire Mark, Philadelphia Contributionship (1857)

5. Firehouse Roadside Marker, Carversville, PA

7. American Fire Mark, Mutual Assurance Co. Philadelphia (1805)

8. American Fire Mark, Fire Association of Philadelphia (1817)

9. American Fire Mark, Insurance Co. of North America (1830)

11. Leather Fire Bucket (1750)

12. Engine House, 100 Block Belmont Ave., Philadelphia, PA

13. Reed Street Fire House, Philadelphia, PA

13. Detail of Philadelphia Coat of Arms

14. Engine #8, Firemens Museum No. 147, 2nd St., Philadelphia, PA

14. Engine No. 6, Belgrade and Huntington Sts., Philadelphia, PA (1875)

15. Washington Hose Co. No. 1, Conshohocken, PA

16. Bristol Fire Co. No. 1, Historic Bldg. 1681

17. Doylestown Fire Co. No. 1, Doylestown, PA

18. Alarm Ring, Pt. Pleasant Fire Co., Point Pleasant, PA

19. Firehouse Roadside Marker, Carversville, PA

20. Eagle Fire Co., New Hope, PA

21. Midway Fire Co., Lahaska, PA

* American Fire Marks were issued by mutual fire insurance companies to home and business owners 178--1850. Made flat and of iron, the marks were hung on buildings in full view to show the buildings were insured.

List of Works

PAGE #

22. Firehouse, Perkasie, PA

22. Sellersville, PA, Former Fire House

23. Phila. Steam Fire Co. No. 1, Pottstown, PA

24. Laurel Fire Company No. 1, York, PA

25. Fire Bell, York Co. Fire Museum, York, PA

26. Royal Fire Station No. 6, York, PA

27. Union Fire Co. No. 1, Carlisle, PA

28. Hook and Ladder No. 1, Reading, PA

28. Engine No. 803, Tremont, PA

29. Dauntless Hook and Ladder, Selinsgrove, PA

30. Washington Fire Co., Ashland, PA

31. Citizens Engine House No. 2, South Williamsport, PA

32. Firehouse, Shartlesville, PA

33. Marion Hose Co. No. 1, Jim Thorpe, PA

34. Marion Fire Co., Stouchsburg, PA

35. Anthracite Fire Co., Mt. Carmel, PA (1882)

36. Relief Hose Company No. 2, Raritan, NJ

36. Atlantic City Fire Dept., Engine No. 4, Truck No. #4, Atlantic City, NJ

37. Cape May Fire Museum, Cape May, NJ

38. Freehold Fire Dept., Freehold, NJ

38. West-End Hose Co., Somerville, NJ (1888)

List of Works

PAGE #

39. Fire Headquarters, South Orange, NJ

40. Jersey City Fire Dept., Truck No. 4, Jersey City, NJ

41. Hook and Ladder No. 3, Central Ave., Jersey City, NJ

41. Engine Company 5, Jersey City, NJ

42. Hoboken Ladder Co., Hoboken, NJ

43. Fire Station and Town Hall, Bordentown, NJ

44. Relief Fire Engine Co. No. 1, Mt. Holly, NJ

45. Engine Company No. 5, Trenton, NJ

46. Fleetwing Fire Co., Lambertville, NJ

47. Hibernia Fire House, Lambertville, NJ

48. Edgewater Vol. Fire Dept., Edgewater, NJ

49. Firehouse, Phillipsburg, NJ

50. Junior Fire Co. No. 2, Frederick, MD

51. Engine No. 6, Fire Museum, Baltimore, MD

52. United Fire Co. No. 3, Frederick, MD

53. Engine 55, 363 Broome Street, NY

54. Hook and Ladder #8, Varick St., New York, NY

55. New York Fire Dept., 163 East 67th St., New York, NY

56. Engine 4 Firehouse, Elmira, NY

57. Firemans Hall, Kingston, NY (1857); Eagle Hook and Ladder No. 1; Washington No. 3 on Fair St., Kingston, NY

List of Works

PAGE #

58. A.M. Osborn Hose Co., Catskill, NY

59. Brick Firehouse, Catskill, NY

60. C.H. Evans Fire Co., Hudson, NY

61. J.W. Hoysradt Hose & Chemical Co., Hudson, NY

62. H.W. Rogers Hose Co. No. 2, Hudson, NY

63. Central Fire Station, Cortland, NY

64. Engine No. 6, Waterbury Fire Dept., Waterbury, CT

65. Citizens Engine Co. No. 2, Seymour, CT

66. Worcester Fire Dept., Worcester, MA

67. Central Fire Division on Commercial St., Worcester, MA

68. Lowell Fire Dept., Lawrence St. Station 1891

69. Torrent Fire House, Lowell, MA, on Branch St., Ladder No. 2 (1877)

70. Firehouse, Ipswich, MA

71. Massasoit Fire Company, Damariscotta, ME

72. Paris Fire Dept., Paris, ME

73. Auburn Engine House, Auburn, ME

74. Fire House, Thomaston, ME

75. Engine House No. 4, Racine, WI

76. Engine 24, Oakland, CA